A COURSE in COURAGE

Disarming
the Darkness with
Strength of Heart

....

**As told through JOHN McKIBBIN
to GATES McKIBBIN**

LIFELINES LIBRARY

For information, contact:

Field Flowers, Inc.
641 Healdsburg Avenue
Healdsburg, CA 95448
707 433 9771
www.fieldflowers.com
www.lifelineslibrary.com

Cover and text design by Kajun Design

Front cover detail from "Water Serpents I"
by Gustav Klimt (Erich Lessing/Art Resource)

Author's photo by Christina Schmidhofer

ISBN 1-929799-02-0

Printed with soy-based ink on recycled paper,
30% post-consumer

To Ferces Duet, the most courageous messenger of spirit I know

What began three years ago as a series of journal entries is now coming into the world as a series of books. All along the way people with the perspective and expertise I needed crossed my path at exactly the right time. Each person has contributed soul and substance to the project. I am abundantly grateful to:

- ◆ **Ned Engle**, who saw what my writings could become long before I did and then adroitly guided me there.

- ◆ **Barbra Dillenger**, **Michael Makay**, **Benjo Masilungan** and **Anthony Corso**, whose comments on each new manuscript reassured me of the accuracy and usefulness of the material.

- ◆ **Judith Appelbaum** and **Florence Janovic** at Sensible Solutions, whose savvy counsel about the publishing industry kept me confident and on course.

- ◆ **Carol Fall**, who offered discerning marketing advice and was the creative force behind the book titles.

- ◆ **Erin Blackwell** and **Cynthia Rubin**, whose editorial finesse honored and strengthened the messages.

- ◆ **Laurie Smith** and **Pat Koren** at Kajun Design, who transformed each book into a jewel within and without.

Also by Gates McKibbin:

The Light in the Living Room: Dad's Messages from the Other Side

LoveLines: Notes on Loving and Being Loved

A Handbook on Hope: Fusing Optimism and Action

The Life of the Soul: The Path of Spirit in Your Lifetimes

Available Wisdom: Insights from Beyond the Third Dimension

CONTENTS

GLOSSARY

Creation consists of multiple dimensions of reality. Each dimension is characterized by its vibratory or magnetic quality. The higher the frequency at which the dimension vibrates, the more at one it is with God. The **higher realms** are the dimensions of spiritual reality beyond the material world, where distinctions based on time and space do not exist.

Karma is composed of imprints on your soul created by your choices (thoughts, words and actions). Choices that embrace spirit heal, balance, complete and remove karmic imprints from your current and prior lifetimes that distance your soul from God. Choices that deny or avoid spirit add new imprints that must be healed, balanced, completed and removed later.

Your **lesson** is the larger karmic pattern or theme you are addressing during this lifetime.

Your **mission** is the major contribution you are making in this lifetime to enable the evolution of collective consciousness toward oneness with God.

Your **soul** is the vessel for your spirit. It carries an

2

infinite variety of karmic imprints that record the experiences your spirit has had, in and out of embodiment. Your soul is all love and light. It represents your limitless potential to embrace spirit to the fullest capacity.

Spirit guides are spiritual entities who have committed to helping you follow the path of love and contribute to the spiritual evolution of all creation. They whisper in your ear telepathically. They send you insights and intuitive flashes. They reaffirm your deepest inner knowing that there is a benevolent higher power inherent in all things.

The **third dimension** is the material reality on planet earth. It consists of dense physical matter that vibrates slowly. The third dimension is characterized by segmented linear time (past, present and future) and compartmentalized space (measurements, boundaries and separation).

The **veil** is a magnetic field surrounding planet earth that separates the vibratory capacity of the third dimension from that of the higher realms. It forms a barrier between your earthly awareness and your higher consciousness. The veil creates the illusion that material reality—and your survival in it—is your reason for being.

The term **we** that is used throughout this book refers to John McKibbin, the spirit who was Gates' father in this lifetime, and the other spiritual entities collaborating with him on the messages he sent down to her.

The COURAGE to DISARM DARKNESS

The messages that follow were channeled through my deceased father, John McKibbin, to me from the other side of the veil. They compose the third of six books in the LifeLines Library that he sent down between 1996 and 1999.

The use of the term *darkness* in this book is not linked with the yielding, interior feminine as it is defined in some spiritual philosophies. Nor is it synonymous with the Jungian shadow side. Rather, darkness is defined here as the weakening of love and light in any aspect of your life.

This volume reveals the myriad detours darkness creates on your journey to spirit. Here you will find the information you need to navigate minefields of darkness with courage and awareness. You will be able to recognize darkness and neutralize its influence more quickly when it interrupts your life.

Darkness is a sly adversary. It disguises itself in many different cloaks—anger, cynicism, arrogance, flattery—to access an area of vulnerability within you. Sometimes it attacks your sense of inadequacy, sometimes your sense of superiority.

Uncommon courage is required to move beyond the influence of darkness. Courage requires enduring strength of heart—which is love, or spirit. The word *courage* derives from *coeur,* meaning "heart" in French, from the Latin *cor.*

The first step toward courage involves assessing your current reality. You must name the unnameable, face your deepest fears, address your most profound hypocrisies and unmask your most ingrained sources of despair. You cannot move through and then beyond these barriers to spirit if you are not willing to see them exactly as they are. More courage is required in this initial phase than in almost any other, so tenacious is the desire to deny the darkness rather than confront it.

Next you must go deep within yourself to uncover the origin of your most penetrating inner light. Perhaps it emerges from a healthy relationship with a spouse, partner, family member or friend. Perhaps it derives from an unshakable religious conviction. Perhaps it arises from your ability to love someone unconditionally.

Whatever the wellspring, you must affirm your ability to love. Recall when you acted with courage against difficult odds. Remember times when your empathy and generosity led you to give selflessly to another. Remind yourself how the power of love has been a catalyst for you to be and do far more than you had thought possible.

Then, with the shield of your awareness of darkness and the sword of your inner knowing, move into the darkness. Acknowledge its existence. Recognize the role it has played in your life. Declare your decision to disarm its influence over you.

Do not pretend that the darkness does not exist or shrink from its threats. Rather, remain true to your heart and your light-filled self, no matter how lacking in light you find the people and circumstances that surround you.

- *Be love,* even when others refuse or do not know how to act with love.
- *Be love,* even when others resist you with all their might.
- *Be love,* even when your ego tells you that you are a fool.

Your ability to be love amidst opposition is the measure of your courage.

Strength of heart is a gift of spirit. Courage follows the path of light—honesty, integrity and forgiveness. For within the heart dwells spirit. And spirit-based actions prevail over spirit-less ones, maybe not immediately or easily, but eventually—eternally.

Act from that base of inner power. Understand that courage ultimately requires your refusal to participate in and perpetuate the dynamics of darkness. For to conquer through deviousness and force is to strengthen the means of darkness. When you see darkness for what it is—the weakening of spirit—and choose to fill yourself with its opposite, you negate its ability to limit and intimidate you.

The fact that this book is in your hands is indication enough that you are already committed to choosing light over its opposite. May these messages guide you and reaffirm your strength of heart.

COURAGE

You can sustain your strength of heart in these ways:

♦ Pray for peace, but also live it with every step you take and every smile you smile.

♦ Speak of love but more importantly, be love.

♦ Intend the best for others, but recognize that they alone influence the direction of their lives.

♦ Care from the depths of your heart, but do so unconditionally.

♦ Look forward, but also remain involved in the present.

♦ Look back, but do so with acceptance and gratitude.

♦ Rise above your own difficulties, but do not judge others for their inability to accomplish the same.

♦ Be flexible and resilient, but do so from a firm foundation in spirit.

♦ See God in all that is, but do not neglect to see God within yourself.

♦ Speak your truth, but refrain from trying to convince others of it.

- Carry the torch of love, but do not be dismayed when others cannot see it.
- Remember that you may walk in the shadows and lose your way. But you will find it again. You need not be lost for long.

MANIFESTATIONS of DARKNESS

Darkness is the absence of light, the dimming of spirit, the diminishing of love. It exists in varying degrees within you and in the interpersonal environment that surrounds you. Darkness pulls you away from joy and leads you to despair. To live in darkness is to imbibe only tiny sips of spirit. To embody darkness is to feel bereft of the inner resources you need to soar and thrive.

You must deal with darkness in two general areas of your life: within yourself and in the context in which you live and function in the third dimension.

Darkness within you manifests as feelings, beliefs, values or thought patterns that extinguish love in your life.

- Darkness is inherent in *feelings* of fear, hatred, frustration, anxiety, powerlessness and hopelessness.
- Darkness stimulates *beliefs* that separate people and the rest of creation into categories such as good and evil, beautiful and ugly, worthy and worthless.
- *Values* that reinforce darkness encourage greed,

selfishness, aggression, dishonesty, competition and control.

♦ *Thought patterns* of darkness include manipulation, hypocrisy and discrimination.

When you experience yourself exhibiting any of these forms of darkness, you must release them. This release might be neither immediate nor complete. You probably will have to revisit the darkness many times until you have uprooted it at its source. You must refrain from judging yourself negatively because the darkness has come into your life. It is human to experience it; it is divine to choose to unshackle yourself from it.

Darkness is seductive. It has an uncanny ability to target your vulnerabilities. It can pinpoint your weaknesses and blind spots. Darkness in your everyday life cannot be eliminated or even avoided. But it can be handled with conscious awareness when you encounter it.

Understand that darkness is an inherent part of God's plan. Without it there would be no challenges to spirit, and therefore no catalysts for your spiritual growth.

From DARKNESS
to LIGHT

To be human is to struggle with darkness. To evolve spiritually is to move away from the influence of darkness and embrace the light.

You are enticed with endless opportunities to disown your spirit for instant rewards, ego gratification or increased control over others. This happens each time you make a choice, whether you are conscious of it or not. And each choice either affirms light or strengthens darkness.

How does darkness reveal itself in everyday life? You'd be surprised at its far-reaching influence. Recall a day in your own life.

You awake to the sound of horns honking. People are impatient, in a rush to get to work. You tell yourself (self-righteously) how inconsiderate some people are.

You have just let in a little darkness.

At the office a co-worker stops by to complain about someone in another department. You agree, adding your own stories about how incompetent she is. Soon you are both indignant. The delays you have been experiencing are irrefutably her fault. You agree that she deserves to be called on the carpet.

You have just let in a little darkness.

Then you get a phone call from a business associate you have been avoiding. He wants to get together for dinner when he is in town. You'd rather not. You know that you have nothing scheduled on the evening in question, but you tell him that you have a commitment you cannot cancel. You promise to get together with him next time.

That's more darkness.

That same day you get angry at an airline ticket agent, gossip about a friend, use an expired bus transfer, betray a confidence and walk blindly by a number of homeless people asking for assistance. Each one of these acts erodes a bit of light and adds a bit of darkness.

On each occasion you could have made a different choice. You could have affirmed spirit. Instead, you chose judging and anger, impatience and avoidance.

Darkness may take the form of divisive competitiveness. It may consist of physical or psychological violence. It may manifest as prejudice or persecution. It may arise as greed or selfishness. Whatever the venue for darkness, you are living in a cauldron of it.

It is a formidable task to transcend such forces—to choose love.

Do not expect others to understand your actions when that is your choice. Some of them will believe you are an inexperienced innocent or a kooky eccentric. Others may explain reality as they see it so you can be more "realistic." Although they may be motivated by the best of intentions, they may be convincing you to swim with the tide of darkness rather than against it.

Sometimes people experience your light as a threat. It challenges the status quo that is maintained by darkness. The further into darkness the people around you fall, the more forcibly they will try to take you with them. Remember that. Do not underestimate their power. Do not discount their intentions. They will be focused on their own survival at any cost.

How do you engage with them and maintain your integrity?

First you must be absolutely certain about what you believe and value. Draw the line beyond which you will not step, then refuse to step beyond it.

- What do you value?
- What aspects of your self are you committed to honoring?
- What are you not willing to compromise?
- How flexible are you willing to be?
- When is inflexibility the only option?

Now take a look at your answers to these questions as they relate to a particular situation.

- To what extent are your actions rooted in unconditional love, non-judging and detachment?
- Do they affirm spirit in yourself and others?

Next, test a spirit-based approach in a dark situation with low risk. Hold your ground against the sorcery that surrounds you. Be light, even in the most impossible or incongruous surroundings. If you cannot do that, walk away. Whatever you do, refrain from engaging with or participating in the dynamics of darkness.

If this approach overwhelms you, separate the situation into its individual aspects. Maybe you are in a group of people who are undermining each other and thus the group's effectiveness. Is there one person with whom you can share your light without seeing it immediately extinguished? If so, connect with that person, if only for a moment, to smile or share a positive comment.

Contemplate the following:

- Unconditional love is the most powerful antidote to the forces of darkness, which have no means of counteracting it.
- You are never required to be subservient to darkness, no matter how pervasive or overwhelming it is, for your light can always overcome darkness.
- It is impossible to beat the darkness at its win/lose game. You only increase darkness when you do that. Use your light as a scythe—not a sword.
- When you become more conscious of the realities you face and the choices you make, you can then shift them toward light and love.
- The more you act from love, the more you threaten darkness. Its response to these threats is to find ever more compelling ways to draw you away from the light. But the more powerful your love becomes, the more you overcome your fears.
- When you create a light-infused situation, darkness cannot dwell within it. Act with clarity of purpose and the courage of your convictions. Forgive instead of blaming; refrain from judging; avoid the clutches of fear and anger; maintain your humanity and kindness.
- Become more aware of your choices. Each one. All day. Every day. Then make them more loving.

No act of love, no matter how apparently insignificant, is lost.

The PEARL of GREAT PRICE

Embedded within you are many treasures, all of them gifts from God. One of the greatest treasures of all is the pearl of great price. What is the pearl and what is the price? The pearl is inner knowing—the awareness of the God-force within. The price is the struggle it takes to unearth this knowing—the dark night of the soul from which the spirit is reborn.

The pearl of great price cannot be given. It must be earned. It cannot be found by accident or handed to you as a result of the experiences or teachings of another. It is not available for purchase or trade. It cannot be measured or appraised. It has value to no one but you. It is within you always, yet does not reveal itself until you have found the source of your own perpetual light.

How do you go about earning it? Most of the time this happens when you find yourself in a situation leading to darkness and difficulty. You would not choose to be there because it is so agonizing, but once you are, you find that the most effective way out is the path of spirit. As you overcome the trauma and embrace spirit, you discover the pearl—a pulsating iridescent globe of life and light and love. It is God within you.

But you do not have to wait until dire circumstances force you to plumb the depths of your inner being. You can decide at any point to face your greatest fears and address the sources of your most entrenched resistance.

Think about your life at this moment. Now ask yourself the following questions, and answer them as honestly as you can:

- What am I avoiding most strenuously?
- When do I quake the most?
- What makes me feel the most insecure or inadequate?
- What potential failure do I worry about the most?
- How do I most effectively sabotage myself?
- What do I dread more than anything else?

Consider your responses. What patterns do you see? If you could identify one aspect of yourself that underlies all of your answers, what would it be? Do you have the capacity to transform it? What would the first step be? What would you be risking? What would you be gaining? Do you have the courage to move into and through this unknown?

You are loved; you are guided. You will not go into the unknown unaided or without resources. No one can do the work for you or protect you from the turmoil that is likely to result. On the other hand, no one can give you the peace that comes from having come face-to-face with your own limitations and transcended them.

You and you alone can give yourself the pearl of great price. You deserve it. It is yours. It is you.

From FORBIDDING to NON-JUDGING

To forbid is to establish parameters for unacceptable behavior. This requires the establishment of a rule and consequences for its transgression.

To establish rules is to say, "This is valid, and this is not. Therefore, you may do this but not this."

Much is forbidden in your material reality. Those constraints were put in place in order to accommodate the difficulties of living in community.

Society decrees that you may not murder another, steal from another or sexually abuse another. If you do so and are found guilty, you will be punished according to the parameters of the prevailing legal system. Those guidelines for punishment vary from one country to the next and one culture to the next. Some cultures are more ruthless, some more forgiving.

Who is to say whose rules are correct? What is taboo in one culture may be held in the highest regard by another. What was acceptable in ancient times is heresy today. What you consider to be supreme now may be declared pagan in the next 100 or 1,000 years.

When you move into the higher dimensions, you discover that nothing is forbidden. There are no boundaries around anything. There is no list of what you can and cannot do; there are no rules outlining punishment for going astray.

Nothing is forbidden by God in heaven or on earth. God does not judge anyone's thoughts, words or deeds. God also does not punish. God forgives—again and again and again.

God does, however, give you a soul that retains the memory of all of your actions in all of your embodiments. That is your karma—the unremitting requirement to heal, complete and balance past actions with current ones.

How successfully you address your karmic patterns has no bearing on God's ability to forgive. God's is not a conditional forgiveness. You are already forgiven, whether you carry the karma for 10 lifetimes or 10 minutes.

Such a situation is almost unimaginable on the earthly plane. You believe that without laws, rules and social standards, things would spin out of control quickly. People would spend their energies vying for dominion over each other. There would be more extreme differentiation between the haves and the have-nots.

Are things so very different from that now? All of the forbidding that you do does not constrain malevolent behavior.

The issue goes deeper. If something is forbidden, and therefore you do not do it, you are making only a half-choice. The half-choice is to follow the rules, to keep from breaking the law, to avoid punishment.

A whole choice would be to act according to spirit—

to treat another with love or compassion, to give unconditionally, to refrain from causing another harm. A whole
choice would be to do so not because you will be re-
warded if you do or punished if you do not, but because
you are guided by your love—by your light within—to
do so.

When there is no motive other than love, you are act-
ing from your highest consciousness. And when you act
from your highest consciousness, it is not necessary to
forbid anything—ever.

That is the end point of spiritual evolution. It is
available to all.

From TURBULENCE to TRANQUILITY

Turbulence occurs with the warring of light and dark. The greater the turbulence, the more desperate the tug-of-war. The more significant the turbulence, the higher the stakes—and the greater the need for serenity.

To be tranquil is to maintain inner peace amidst this turbulence. Tranquility is not synonymous with stillness, for stillness is a result of non-movement. Tranquility arises from peace.

When light and dark are in combat, tranquility seems an unlikely companion. After all, how can you be at peace when so much struggle surrounds you? Isn't it more suitable to engage in the conflict, the better to see it come to an appropriate end, than to do nothing and adopt the attitude that all is well?

Maintaining tranquility does not require disengagement. You may be required to jump into the turbulence. You may have to invest all of yourself in the struggle. But you do not need to lose your tranquility in the process.

How can you be turbulent and tranquil at the same time?

To answer that question a distinction must be made. You are not turbulent; you are in a turbulent situation. The turbulence is external; tranquility is internal. The two can coexist.

The best way to remain effective during turbulence is to remain tranquil.

- ◆ Tranquility enables you to read the situation with your body, mind and spirit aligned, then act and react accordingly.
- ◆ Tranquility gives you the depth of perception that empowers you to see below the surface conditions of turbulence and redirect the forces of light to overcome the darkness.
- ◆ Tranquility offers you clarity amidst the confusion and optimism amidst the doubt.

When you remain tranquil, the turbulence dies down and eventually ceases. Tranquility can then pervade both within and without.

From CONFLICT
to CONSCIOUSNESS

The forces of darkness have one intention: to overcome the light. They cannot succeed by diverting, blocking or refracting the light. Under those circumstances light still exists, albeit in an altered or compromised form.

Darkness can prevail only if it annihilates the light, and that requires conflict. Darkness must win; light must lose and be obliterated.

Conflict is a necessary part of life. It is an essential dynamic of the universe. To avoid conflict is to allow darkness to have a greater influence than it deserves or demands. To avoid conflict is to strengthen the destructive power of darkness through inaction and implicit consent.

It is not un-spiritual to engage in conflict with darkness. The nature of the conflict is what matters. If your intention is to fight darkness with your own darkness (hate, resistance, punishment), negativity will overtake you and you will gain nothing.

But if your intention is to engage in conflict with

darkness by embracing light, no matter how tenuous the circumstances, you will always prevail. Darkness can never conquer light.

On the one hand, you are God incarnate, with the potentiality of living in peace, harmony and serenity. You are spiritually whole. This part of you draws you to the higher planes, where you can be more, detach more, love more. On some level you know this, though your experience of it may be rare.

On the other hand, you are mortal. You must earn a living, keep a roof over your head, interact with people who may or may not be honorable. Your daily life is filled with anything but peace and harmony. But you are alive; you are materially whole. This part of you insists that you survive first and nurture spirit second. It gives you tasks that fill your days—structuring your time, committing your energy and leaving little room for tending to your soul.

The conflict, then, is between your higher consciousness, which longs to fly free to the spiritual realms, and your body consciousness, which hangs on to material reality with all of its might.

Given this conflict, what are your choices?

- ♦ You can remain unconscious of the conflict.
- ♦ You can pretend that conflict does not exist, even if you are conscious of it.
- ♦ You can allow both voices their due, moving them toward an inner dialogue that might avert conflict.
- ♦ Or you can declare your higher consciousness the more powerful. You can commit to it, dedicate your life to strengthening it and refuse to empower your body consciousness any more than is necessary.

The choice is yours. This is a critical decision—a life-changing one. Do not resist this conflict. Engage the darkness with your love and light, courage and commitment. You will be amazed at how strong—and serene—you can be.

From CATACLYSM to REBIRTH

Cataclysmic events take the measure of your faith—the degree to which you can embody spirit despite sudden crises and chaos.

Cataclysms threaten your ability to retain what you have built over time, be it wealth or status, security or power. They also introduce significant uncertainty into your life. What used to be under your control is now chaotic. When you face a cataclysm—a death or divorce, a financial catastrophe or career derailment—your initial response is to grab hold of anything that might contain your resulting sense of insecurity.

A cataclysm is certainly not something to be welcomed—initially, at least. It sets into motion a series of events that challenge everything you believed to be true about the world and your place in it. But that very challenge is an opportunity to wipe the slate clean and to begin anew, using your wisdom and experience to guide your next steps into the unknown.

Think about what makes something cataclysmic. It is the degree to which your present and future situation are unknown. The greater the depth and breadth of uncertainty, the greater the sense of cataclysm you experience.

When cataclysm strikes, you have two choices. You can accept the new reality it introduces and make the most of having a fresh start, or wring your hands over the trauma of it all. The latter approach will keep you in darkness and fear, convincing you that the outcome can be nothing short of horrid. The former approach will reveal those aspects of your life that you are glad to be rid of and the opportunity you now have to build a new existence.

That may be good in theory, but how can you be opportunistic while everything around you is in tatters?

First, enumerate the aspects of your life that are not changing. You may discover that what is most important to you remains uncompromised. You still have a foundation to build upon, even if it is no more concrete than your values or your faith. That is enough.

Then think of the resources you still have at your disposal. You may at first believe that there are none, but that is an inaccurate perception. You have time and energy, relationships and intelligence, wisdom and optimism. Those will carry you far.

Finally, see uncertainty as a gift rather than a curse.

- ♦ Strengthen your ability to tolerate ambiguity.
- ♦ See the doors that are opening for you as well as the ones that are closing.
- ♦ Send love to yourself and others. You have that in abundance, if nothing else.
- ♦ Create space for fresh perspectives.
- ♦ Acknowledge what is gone and recognize what is about to appear.

Find the jewel embedded in the upheaval.

From MISERY
to MASTERY

You can be in the most luxurious of surroundings and feel miserable. You can live in the most miserable of circumstances and feel joy.

Misery is a function of physical, mental and spiritual starvation. To feed the body inadequately is to weaken your ability to function in the world. That creates the misery of physical weakness, sickness, emaciation and in extreme circumstances, death. Such misery is darkness made manifest in the body. Material poverty also affects your physical health and well-being.

Inadequate food or shelter threaten your very existence and make physical survival a priority.

To feed the mind inadequately is to erode your ability to consider situations with balance, clarity and integrity. It is to resist new perspectives or creative ideas that threaten established perspectives. Intellectual poverty results in mental miseries ranging from dislike to hate, from preference to prejudice, from control to tyranny.

To feed the spirit inadequately is to see and experience despair over joy, scarcity over abundance, limitation over opportunity and abuse over honor. You starve spirit when you cherish opinions, reinforce blame, find fault or create divisiveness. Spiritual poverty is the inability to see through or beyond the darkness that punctuates your existence. It creates waves of doubt and fear; it assumes the worst, whether it is related to character or consequences.

Physical, mental and spiritual deprivation debilitate the influence of love in your life.

To break this cycle of misery is to affirm the power of spirit—no matter how deprived the body and mind may be. Spirit can thrive even in the face of conditions that are physically and mentally intolerable.

Take your spiritual power back. Choose mastery over misery.

MASTERY

To master an art or an intellectual pursuit requires discipline and hard work. It also requires the opposite—relaxation and dexterity.

Think of a renowned chef. That person's creations are extraordinary not just because he or she went to the best culinary academies and learned how to prepare food to meet the exacting principles of fine dining. They are memorable because the chef did that, and then invented subtle new cooking techniques and flavor combinations using the freshest ingredients.

Consider the one area of your life in which you have the greatest skill. First you probably developed exceptional skills, perhaps by combining natural ability with practice. Then as you gained confidence, you began to relax into the doing of it. You replaced trying hard with loosening up.

Mastery lies at that intersection of capability and contentment. You cannot be masterful if you are incompetent. You also cannot be masterful if you are not at peace with yourself.

Mastery in evolving toward the One requires the discipline to access spirit on a regular basis. Extreme measures are not necessary here. Rather, you need only to set aside minutes every day to be with spirit, however you choose. During that time, clear your mind of all thoughts. If you find that you cannot do that, then occupy your mind with thoughts of love and gratefulness. Count your blessings. Acknowledge the grace that surrounds you. Recognize that you are loved. You will find that the more you do this, the better at it you will become. That is one component of the discipline of the spiritual path.

The other one requires you to become more aware of the thoughts, words and deeds that punctuate your day. If you find that your thoughts are becoming negative, shift the pattern by thinking of something positive in your life. If your words tend to derogate yourself or another, start speaking in supportive ways. If your actions are destructive or divisive, choose to create common ground. This is the discipline of living in a way that is fully conscious.

This foundation of discipline, then, enables you to relax into your day rather than attacking it with a vengeance. When you flow with the natural rhythms that surround you, you see opportunities you may not have recognized before; you seize moments that might have otherwise eluded you; you more naturally integrate spirit into who you are and what you do; you experience moments when you are closer to the One than you ever imagined possible.

You become the master of your own destiny by bringing spirit into your life in simple yet profound ways. It is joyfully disciplined art.

From FEAR
to COURAGE

Fear is one of the most destructive emotions you face. It feeds your deepest insecurities and reminds you of your vulnerabilities. It closes off options and creates obstacles to innovative thinking and action. Fear sets up a self-fulfilling prophecy where you anticipate the worst, and (surprise!) it happens. You fear what you cannot do well, and thus might fail at.

What causes fear? Typically its catalyst is the inability to see the bigger picture or the reluctance to believe in a positive outcome. Fear can also be a manifestation of your sense of inadequacy, incompetence or unworthiness. Finally, you fear what you can neither access nor comprehend.

Fear can identify the one area of your life that you still feel uneasy about, then chip away at your faith that you can rise above it. You can even predict the moves fear will make to entice you into its cave. Your familiarity with fear is a blessing, for it enables you to identify areas in your life where your spirit is weak. It is better than radar at locating pockets of darkness.

The next time you experience a wave of fear, try to approach it this way:

+ *Identify its source.* Whatever fear has hooked itself into is clearly something you need to work on, whether you have been willing to admit it or not.
+ *Consider the reasons for your fear.* Is your fear realistic or unfounded? What are you assuming about the situation that may not be true? What additional information do you need? What actions would alleviate your fears?
+ *Identify the worst-case scenario.* What impact would that outcome have on you? Would you survive it?
+ *Contemplate the choices you make that cause fear to arise.* Would you rather make different choices? If not, can you uproot your fear and make peace with the situation?
+ *Approach fear as a valuable source of information about your spiritual vitality.*

You may discover that what you fear is not so horrible after all. You may find the courage to face your fear and neutralize its hold on you. Or you may decide that there are legitimate reasons to be afraid, and take measures to protect yourself.

Fear and courage are relentless adversaries. Affirm your confidence and courage with the actions you take.

Fear succeeds in controlling you with its messages about risk, scarcity and distrust. These messages steer you away from remembering that you are a child of God—that you are loved and protected by the most powerful force in all of creation. You have nothing to fear. Even death can be viewed fearlessly, for in death you become more at one with spirit.

From ANGER
to RELEASE

What creates anger—that most destructive of all emotions? Anger derives from a belief that an injustice has been done.

In the material world, anger often seems justified. Fairness and equity can be measured, albeit often in an arbitrary way. There are standards of justice against which an assertion or an action can be weighed.

In the world of spirit, however, anger is both inappropriate and unnecessary. When you are angry, you are judging someone or something, which leads you away from spirit.

When you get angry, ferociously and self-righteously, you are usually assigning blame, thereby perpetuating the cycle of judging. You think, "That was wrong and I am angry about it." In order to change this pattern, you must recognize that you are blaming and judging.

At that point of recognition, a number of things can happen. You can:

- *Be hypocritical* and pretend not to be angry, treating the perpetrators as if you liked them.

- *Internalize your feelings* and keep your thoughts to yourself but harbor a grudge.
- *Act out* and state your opinion, getting your anger off your chest in a non-abusive way.
- *Be authentic* and speak your truth without judging, then forgive the others for what occurred and yourself for getting angry.

The path of forgiveness is the passage away from anger. When you can forgive, you release all fury and negative opinion. When you cannot forgive, you must find another way to deal with the anger so that it does not destroy you or others over time.

In order of effectiveness:

- To forgive results in an immediate release of anger.
- To let it go results in a conscious release of anger.
- To work it out results in a gradual release of anger.
- To stuff it results in no release of anger.

Anger smothers spirit with intense negativity. It fuels frustration, powerlessness, vengeance and betrayal. Love and anger simply cannot occupy the same space.

To remain angry, whether you are aware of it or not, is to create conditions that mute the light within. To exist in anger is to silence the voice of love. To give in to anger is to sacrifice your enlightened self at the altar of your judgmental self.

From PREJUDICE to OPEN-MINDEDNESS

To act with prejudice is to pre-judge. The spiritual challenge everyone faces is to transcend the tendency to judge people and their actions.

Judging is not synonymous with using good judgment. The latter involves gathering information, weighing options and making the most reasonable choice based on what you know and anticipate. That practice is not unsound—as long as you realize that much of what you are using to inform your judgment is based on third-dimensional understandings and as such is limited.

You make decisions all the time and reasonableness is a good criterion. So to use good judgment as it applies to decision making is to balance head and heart—to be thoughtful and caring.

But by judging people as being right or wrong, good or evil, saintly or diabolical, you establish yourself as the arbiter of a particular hierarchy and each person's status within it. That status, once assigned or determined, tends to remain static. Once judged, the label usually sticks despite evidence to the contrary.

To be prejudiced is to label someone or something based on predetermined frameworks derived from stereotypes, instead of reasonably attempting to gather and review relevant information. Prejudice extrapolates from one to many categories. It declares, for instance, that if you are blonde, then you are shallow, vapid and fun-loving. What a person can feel comfortable asserting about another based on one or two superficial points is quite remarkable.

People pre-judge for convenience and self-protection. Like well-worn habits, prejudices seem to uncomplicate life's complexities. You see someone, your prejudices speak their mind, you make all sorts of generalizations about the individual regarding everything from her intelligence to her taste in music. You shut the door on any additional input. This saves you the time and energy needed for further thought or consideration.

To judge another is not a prerogative that even God assumes. So how can you? To judge another even before you know anything about her is misguided hubris. To recognize another in all of her humanness is to honor her spirit.

Prejudice usually leads to inaccurate conclusions and is always inappropriate. Tend to your prejudices, the better to identify them and then sweep them away when they appear.

LIMITATION

Limitation surrounds you on planet earth. You are constantly judging and being judged based on a sense of limitation. Judging and limitation in tandem drive feelings such as, *I don't have enough* or *Someone didn't do enough* or *The result wasn't good enough* or *The ideas didn't take people far enough.* "Enough" is measured in terms of sufficiency or excellence.

But what if you stopped judging? What if every time you got out your mental yardstick and prepared to assess something, you set it down without using it? What if you were able to witness and experience things in your life without measuring their worth? What if you were able to acknowledge reality, however contrary to your preferences it might be, and say, "Yes, that's the way it is," without passing judgment?

Would you be aware of any limitation? How could you be?

One of the most tenacious sources of limitation comes from judgments you make about yourself. The "enough" gauge is deployed many times a day where you are concerned. If you are never able to do enough or be enough or accomplish enough, how can you find the serenity and peace inherent in each moment? If an inner voice is constantly nagging you to work smarter, walk faster, be happier, where is there room for spirit? If you focus only on your limitations, you will limit yourself—not access the infinite potential inherent within you.

There are no limits to anything. Whatever you see as a limitation is just something you created, or allowed someone else to convince you of, that results in your being and becoming less than you could be. Wherever you see limitation, it is likely that you are not integrating spirit. The best way to transcend your limitations is to embrace spirit.

Whenever you notice that you are seeing limitation rather than possibility, identify the judgments that are keeping you there and release them. Embrace what is, with your eyes open and your heart full of love.

When you replace limitation with love, you will find that there are no limits to who you are—spiritually or otherwise.

RESISTANCE

Resistance results from the fear that a situation may create more loss than gain. The pessimism inherent in your resistance blocks progress by accentuating limitations rather than opportunities. You resist because you prefer another option to the one being proposed, or because you would rather maintain the known than face the unknown.

Resistance is a function of fear, limitation, preference, and a desire for certainty and predictability—all of which keep you from your path.

You may ask, what about evil and hatred and violence—shouldn't they be resisted? Aren't there times when resistance is aligned with spirit and acquiescence is not? Wouldn't it be unenlightened not to resist wrongdoing?

The answer is, it all depends on what is in your head and heart when you resist.

Think of something you are resisting right now. You are probably repeating some version of the following to yourself: "That is the worst thing that could happen.

There is no way I will go along with this. I am unwilling to face such uncertainty. I cannot tolerate this inequitable situation. I know I can prevail if I hang in there."

All of these statements indicate that your resistance is embedded in:

♦ *Judging,* which suggests that one outcome is better than another.

♦ *Competition,* which sets up a win/lose scheme (that you fully intend to win).

♦ *Closed-mindedness,* which protects you from considering other viewpoints.

♦ *Fear,* which reinforces your adverse reaction to risk and uncertainty.

You can resist without succumbing to these attitudes. Let's say that you encounter a circumstance that is doing great harm to others. You decide that you will refuse to uphold such action and will articulate the reasons for your choice. The key here is to act and speak without denouncing another or declaring your own virtue. Your words and deeds must be simple statements of your own truth—not impassioned indictments aimed at convincing people to follow your lead. Nothing more needs to be explained or urged. This form of resistance is an enhancement of your path—not an obstacle to it.

Sometimes the greatest resistance you experience has no identifiable source. You have a sense that something is not quite in alignment with spirit or that a vague potentiality could wreak havoc. When these feelings arise, try to determine if this is the result of a fear or insecurity you have been harboring. If such is the case, take appropriate action to address the root cause of those anxieties. If the feelings are based on judgments or opinions, release them, then reassess the situation. If they arise from your deepest inner knowing, ask for guidance to help you navigate the as-yet-unrevealed.

Resist only when it is appropriate—and in the appropriate ways.

From HYPOCRISY to AUTHENTICITY

To be hypocritical is to misrepresent how you are feeling, what you are thinking or what you are doing in order to disguise what you really feel, think or do. Family, community and cultural expectations make hypocrisy an apparently legitimate alternative. Most people are taught to say something nice even when it is untrue—to tell a "white lie" in order not to offend another. That form of hypocrisy is relatively harmless, although it is usually unnecessary.

More extreme instances of hypocrisy involve complex, calculated maneuverings in order to deceive. They entail gross machinations designed to dupe others—to earn people's trust in order to take advantage of it, or to lie about circumstances in order to avoid scrutiny.

Hypocrisy erodes your authenticity like waves washing over a rock. An isolated instance of misrepresentation in the context of consistent truthfulness will have little impact. But ongoing hypocrisy warps your sense of truth and falsity. What is false you represent as being true. You lose your bearings in the sea of falsity. There are no fixed stars of authenticity from which you can navigate. Eventually you accept falsity as truth.

You live in an upside-down world, where fact is fiction and fiction is fact. Light is dark and dark is light. The illusion perpetuated by hypocrisy becomes the accepted reality, which only leads to more hypocrisy.

To break the cycle of hypocrisy, assess its value to you:

- Why are you being inauthentic?
- What does it accomplish for you and others?
- How damaging—or damning—would the truth be?
- Could you embrace your truth fully without articulating it to anyone but yourself?
- Must you speak your truth? Perhaps so.
- If you do not speak your truth, is your silence hypocritical? Does it indicate assent where dissent is your truth—or vice versa?
- What is it about the situation that apparently requires you to be deceitful?
- Is it really worth maintaining?
- If not, how can you extricate yourself from your hypocrisy?

Hypocrisy weaves a tangled web. That web is of your own making and your own choosing. Why work so hard to convince others that your opinion, perspective or reality is other than what it actually is? Is there truly no other option? Rarely is that the case.

Come to terms with all of the hypocrisy in your life. You are likely to find it lurking everywhere in the form of:

- Superficial friendships that you maintain out of habit

- Dysfunctional relationships you pretend are healthy
- Dependence masking itself as independence
- Half-hearted agreement to conceal disagreement
- The illusion of trust that hides mistrust

All of this is hypocrisy. You must deal with it honestly, courageously and sincerely.

From TRIBALISM
to COMMUNITY

You tend to think of tribes as ancient cultures or exotic groups in distant locales. But tribes are all around you—ghetto street gangs and college sororities and fraternities, institutional bureaucracies and sports franchises, the Boy Scouts and corporations.

Tribalism creates two categories of people based on their membership in the group. Insiders belong, outsiders do not. Insiders, by way of their involvement with the tribe, are expected to acquire qualities that conform to tribal preferences and traditions. Outsiders may exhibit none of those qualities. It is heresy for insiders not to have them; it is heresy for outsiders to have them.

Of course, the minute you create the distinction between insiders and outsiders, you reside in difference rather than unity. Difference becomes the reason for the tribe's existence. It communicates, "We are distinctive; therefore, we are better."

This is the essence of the we/they dichotomy.

But tribalism goes deeper than that. Not only must insiders prove that they are worthy of being accepted, they must also become the tribe. They lose their individuality. They sacrifice the freedom to think independently, behave differently and challenge authority. Values and beliefs, behaviors and language are prescribed.

In the all-or-nothing tribal world, you are the tribe and all that it represents. You define yourself in terms of something outside of yourself.

The first thing you sacrifice in your search for acceptance is your uniqueness. In your pursuit of commonality you lose your individuality.

Prescriptions dictate; norms normalize; frameworks imprison. Each attempt you make to fit external definitions of who you are compromises your internal sense of who you are. Finally you lose sight of your soul. You and the tribal oversoul are one.

Heighten your awareness of the tribes in which you have official or unofficial membership.

- ♦ What have you given away for that membership?
- ♦ What have you acquired in return?
- ♦ Are the benefits of belonging worth the cost to you?
- ♦ On what basis are people excluded? Is that legitimate?
- ♦ Are you in a position to cancel your membership in the group if you so choose?

From PUNISHMENT to HONOR

To punish is to judge actions as negative and then seek to balance those actions with an equal measure of negativity. To punish is to indicate that you choose revenge over forgiveness, hate over love, divisiveness over unity. To punish is to feed darkness rather than annihilate it.

What does that accomplish? Nothing positive, to be sure.

Why, then, is punishment so integral to the laws of human society? For every crime there is a punishment. It may not be meted out until the person is proven guilty, but once that proof is established, punishment ensues. You accept as an unquestioned tenet of civilized society that the punishment should suit the crime. So you make some people prisoners and execute others. Those who are released from imprisonment are labeled criminals, ensuring a lifetime of punishment despite their having supposedly paid their debt to society.

What does this system of punishments accomplish? Does it reduce crime? Does it stop people from stealing from each other or killing each other? Does it make the world a better place? Does it affirm spirit in everyone?

How could it?

Punishment recognizes only the darkness in others and their actions, then answers that darkness with more darkness. How can compounding a negative create a positive? How can punishment result in progress? How can vengeance right a wrong?

You could support the evolution of spirit both individually and collectively if instead of punishing you established opportunities for:

♦ Healing the spirit

♦ Empowering individual competence

♦ Releasing the bondage of despair and replacing it with hope

♦ Affirming the value and beauty within each person

You are on earth to honor spirit in yourself and others—not to destroy it.

Choose to reaffirm spirit even in the face of the most despicable deeds—especially in the face of the most despicable deeds. How else can the light prevail?

From CYNICISM
to OPTIMISM

So many aspects of the modern world embody cynicism. Tabloids manufacture photos, label them with sensationalist headlines, then represent the product as fact. Many people who buy these publications know that they are reading fiction dressed up as fact. Nonetheless, they treat it as if it were true. Illusion replaces reality. Few are fooled by it, including those who create it, those who indulge in it and those who profit by it.

That is cynicism.

Cynicism and idealism are two sides of the same coin. The idealistic worldview is that:

- ♦ Effortlessly, miraculously, inevitably the weaknesses of human nature will be overcome by the good inherent in everyone.
- ♦ Higher consciousness will predominate over a more limited sense of existence.
- ♦ People always opt for selflessness over self-interest.
- ♦ Generosity will prevail over greed, and long-term investment in the greater good will surmount short-term gain for the few.

Such idealism is welcome, for it acknowledges the existence of spirit in all people. But it is also naïve, for it refuses to admit the unenlightened aspects of human nature. Idealism is neither realistic nor viable.

Cynicism is also unrealistic. It assumes that people focus only on what benefits them, no matter what harm it may cause others. It argues that because everyone else is out to grab as much for themselves as possible, you are a fool if you do not do the same thing for yourself.

Cynicism acknowledges only the dark side of human nature. It intimates, "Why even try to be loving, thoughtful or generous if what you get in return is someone taking advantage of you? You are either the aggressor or the victim. Better to be on the offense than the defense. That way you acquire more and never need to apologize."

Your choice, however, is not between cynicism and idealism, for neither offers a reasonable guide to behavior. Idealism ends inevitably in disillusionment with human nature—the recognition that limitation and scarcity influence action as much as potential and abundance do. Cynicism begins with the recognition of limitation and scarcity, then moves from there to even more deeply ingrained negative perspectives on human existence.

Instead, you can make a clear-headed assessment of the people in the circumstances that surround you. Always look for the spark of spirit, even in the darkest encounters, and do everything in your power to enhance it in yourself and others.

Build your ability to read the undercurrents in every situation—the trade-offs and tugs-of-war. Do not expect people who are out for themselves to be compassionate and generous. At the same time, do not expect people to necessarily be out for themselves and therefore incapable of true caring.

Everyone is spirit in all its glory. Everyone is also a survivor leading a tenuous material existence. Everyone has the capacity to be both selfless and selfish.

To be either an idealist or a cynic is to discount a significant aspect of what it means to be human. Either extreme places you in a vortex of self-perpetuating negativity. Instead, try engaging in self-perpetuating optimism.

TEMPTATION

The word *temptation* makes you think immediately of the Garden of Eden and original sin—and hot fudge sundaes. The socially accepted understanding is that temptation involves desiring something forbidden, and that when one yields to temptation, the result is his or her spiritual downfall.

But what if nothing were forbidden? What if there were absolutely no hard and fast guidelines about the right or wrong behavior? What if you could give in to temptation whenever you wanted and not be judged negatively for it or be damned because of it?

That is, of course, the case. Nothing in all of God's creation is forbidden.

Something is a temptation if your indulgence in it costs more than the benefit you derive from experiencing it. Be aware, however, of the definition of "cost." If it is a socially-imposed parameter, it may or may not be a cost to you on your own spiritual path. Yes, you do live in a culture with entrenched norms and yes, you do need to honor those norms in order to support the smooth running of society. But if those norms run contrary to your soul's evolution, then the cost to you spiritually is greater than the cost to you socially. You must never sacrifice spirit for social acceptance.

What is a temptation, then? It is something that draws you away from light and love. It seduces you into judging, anger and betrayal. It causes you to sacrifice the good of the many for the benefit of the few. It convinces you that a brief pleasure is worth the long-term consequences. It is any stimulus that takes you off the path to the One.

Whether its source is a cultural predilection or a personality trait, temptation gives you a powerful opportunity to make a conscious choice that reaffirms spirit. The next time you are tempted to demean another, choose not to. When you are tempted to join others in apportioning blame, refuse to. If you think you cannot live without the latest new gadget, think again. Ditto for the hot fudge sundae.

We are not suggesting that to remain on the path you must live as an ascetic, for to run away from temptation is not the same as overcoming it. We are saying that you must be conscious of the choices you make, whether they involve an impulse purchase or an act of forgiveness. Remember that nothing is forbidden. Everything is available to you—in abundance. What you choose to bring into your life, and how you deal with it once it is there, is the essence of the spiritual challenge.

Temptation is put in your path not so that you can prove that you can avoid what is socially forbidden, but so that you can choose on your own to embody love, uncompromisingly, whatever the circumstances, whatever the constraints, whatever the costs. That is what it means to rise above temptation.

From CORRUPTION to INTEGRITY

To corrupt is to allow the seeds of darkness to take root in the fertile soil of the soul. To corrupt is to choose one's own selfish interests over the greater good, without considering the cost to others. To corrupt is to embolden the worst aspects of human nature, giving them credence and viability.

You equate corruption with despotism, organized crime, blackmail and bribery. This deal-making is corrupt to the core. It is openly acknowledged as being corrupt.

But other, less extreme forms of corruption also damage spirit. Think of what you exchange on a day-to-day basis to survive in the world. At times you have exchanged your honesty, integrity, authenticity, values and inner truth for a less controversial existence in a world where these qualities are compromised. You walked away from your spirit in order to survive. You became corrupt.

And with each act of corruption, whether a small instance of dishonesty or a more significant betrayal, darkness gained a greater foothold within you. Each act of corruption became both easier and more difficult.

Easier in that the greater the darkness, the more room there was for corruption. More difficult in that each corrupt act was done with some awareness that you were slaying an aspect of spirit.

At times you have chosen not to enter into circumstances that demanded such corruption. At other times you have experienced them in all of their irony and agony, then rejected them. You continue to be enticed at times by corrupt people and situations. Sometimes you even create the corruption yourself.

Whatever the source, the key is to remain aware of the dynamics of corruption, and when you recognize them, refuse to participate. What are those dynamics? Here are some examples:

- An opportunity to gain more than your share, more than you have earned or deserve
- A promise that such unfair profit is available with minimal repercussions and risk to yourself and others
- A requirement to withhold information, support, trust or any other spirit-based aspect of yourself
- The loss of personal power—your own or another's
- The affirmation that the benefits of corruption will far outweigh the costs
- The enticement of even greater pleasures and advancements beyond the initial ones promised by corruption

Understand the short-term draw of the corrupt mentality. Give it neither energy nor credence.

From OPPRESSION to STRENGTH

Oppression has existed since the beginning of human civilization on planet earth, manifesting as the relentless abuse of one group by another. A necessary pre-condition of oppression is that one segment of society wield considerably more power than another. Oppression in the extreme occurs when one group holds all the power and the others hold none.

To be powerless is to be required to do the bidding of another, to live without freedoms or to face constant threat to life and limb. To be powerless is to be forced to engage in acts of depravity that shriek the message that there is no God.

That is oppression.

More subtle examples of oppression exist as well. Physical, sexual and psychological abuse are oppressive. So are racism and classism. The underlying assumption is that one group has fewer rights than another, regardless of what the law says. Such attitudes assume that the oppressed will not rise up in protest because they have nowhere to go—no one to turn to.

That is oppression.

The dark side dominates in oppression. It violates spirit, but it does not eradicate it.

Oppression is never acceptable and should never be tolerated—implicitly or explicitly. The only way to deal with oppression is to:

- Identify it openly and declare its existence
- Describe the havoc that it wreaks to the mind, body and spirit
- Resist the oppressors nonviolently
- Force the issue again and again
- Act from love, not judging
- Heal, strengthen, bless and love the oppressed
- Forgive and love the oppressors

From FLATTERY
to HONESTY

Positive feedback feels good, doesn't it? It reaffirms that someone appreciates something about you, whether it is a physical characteristic or a unique ability. There is nothing wrong with such affirmations, is there?

No, there is not—as long as you are clear about the difference between compliments and flattery.

A compliment consists of authentic feedback from someone about how much you are appreciated. Its sole purpose is to communicate something positive to you. Flattery, on the other hand, involves a lack of authenticity, whether in what someone says or why. The contents of the message may be far from what the person actually believes is true. It may be manipulative—said so that the hearer will behave in a certain way because he or she has been flattered.

Genuineness marks the difference between compliments and flattery. How can you distinguish between them? Here are some cues:

♦ Is the message you are hearing from the heart or the head? Words from the heart cannot be manufactured, although they can be faked. Words from the head can be manufactured, although that does not automatically make them inauthentic.

- How vulnerable are you to flattery? Do you need it to feel good about yourself? Do you change your opinions of others based on the nice things they say about you? The more these last two situations are in play, the more likely someone is to use flattery to influence you.

- How much do you flatter others? The more you dish it out, the more you are likely to get it back. Others may ask themselves why they should be genuine with you when you are not being genuine with them.

- What kinds of comments really matter to you? Would you rather be told how someone sees you as a human being or how you appear on the surface?

- Do you prefer honest feedback, even though it may be negative, or would that be too devastating? If so, you may be setting the stage for flattery.

Whatever the intentions and actions of others, you have a responsibility to avoid the tempting trap of flattery, whether as bestower or recipient. Choose not to flatter others, regardless of how much they long for it how it might benefit you. Choose to recognize flattery when it comes your way and let it float on by.

WINNING

Most people have difficulty resisting a win/lose challenge. The ego gratification inherent in winning offers seductive self-assurance. So does the admiration of others, the acclamation and the profit involved.

The assumption behind the adage "To the victor go the spoils" is that after a battle, whatever belonged to the vanquished becomes the property of the conqueror. The victorious ones take possession of the losers' wealth, property, heritage and even dignity.

A different perspective on winning and losing is that losers are powerless only if they give their power over to the victors. Here the term *power* refers to the essential and ultimate source of power—oneness with spirit. You are never required to give that away, just as you can never be forced to deny your integrity or worth.

What value does winning afford you? And whether you win or lose, what harm might you create? Is it worth the potential cost? If you were to win, would you expect to receive more than material gain as a benefit of winning?

Gates McKibbin never imagined that after spending twenty years as a corporate executive, management consultant and adjunct college professor specializing in strategic and organizational renewal, she would publish messages channeled from her deceased father, John McKibbin. For most of her adult life she had balanced a fulfilling professional career and a fascinating spiritual quest. Then quite unexpectedly her father, who visited the earth plane frequently after his death, began sending telepathic messages for her to write in her journal.

Three years and six books later, Gates has now added "Inspirational author and speaker" to her resume. She still helps business executives navigate turbulent change, and she also seeds the planet with insights from the spirit world. To complement the LifeLines Library, Gates has developed a collection of thematic LifeLines note pads featuring her favorite one-liners from the books.

Born and raised in central Illinois, Gates now resides in San Francisco. Whenever she has a few hours of free time, she hunts for vintage jackets, walks to North Beach restaurants for risotto, creates bead-bedecked greeting cards and, of course, continues her journal writing. Gates holds a Ph.D. from the University of Illinois and has received numerous academic awards, among them Phi Beta Kappa.